The BUMPER SEARCH and FIND Activity Book

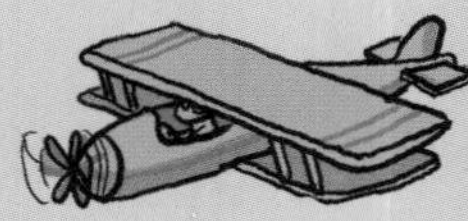

QEB

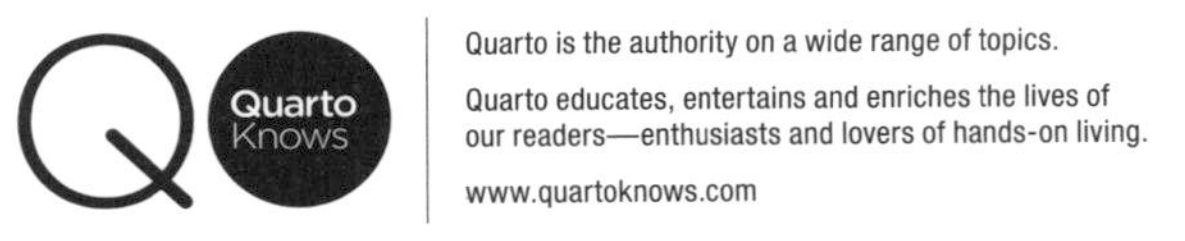

Designed and edited by: Starry Dog Books Ltd

First Published in 2018 by QEB Publishing,
an imprint of The Quarto Group.
6 Orchard Road, Suite 100
Lake Forest, CA 92630
T: +1 949 380 7510
F: +1 949 380 7575
www.QuartoKnows.com

A CIP record for this book is available from the Library of Congress.

ISBN 978 1 68297 332 5

Manufactured in Guangdong China CC112017

MIX
Paper from responsible sources
FSC™ C104723

9 8 7 6 5 4 3 2 1

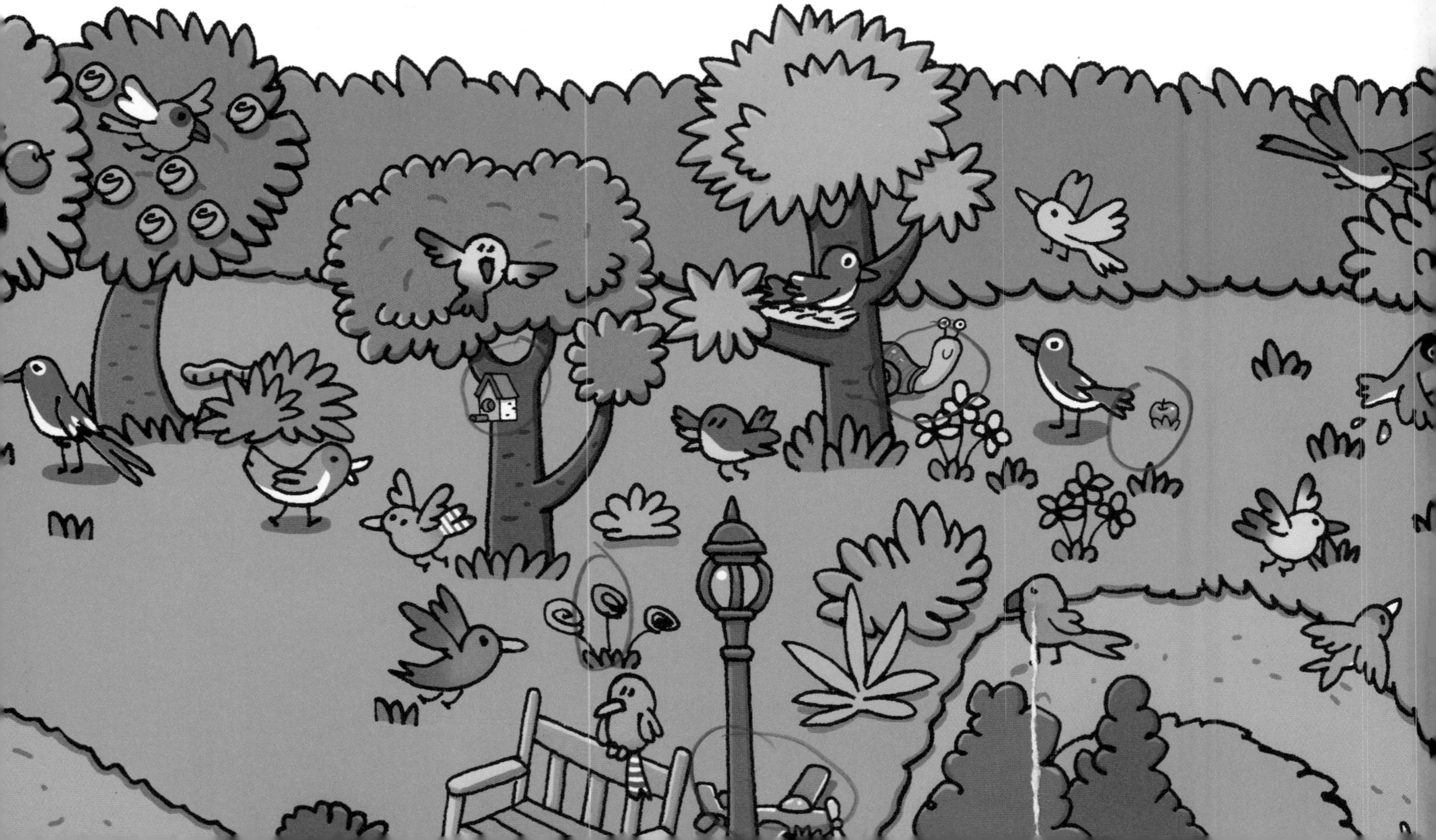

Contents

Can you spot these things?
plane
apple
bird house
flower
snail

Fun on the farm!
There's lots going on. Come and see!
Farmhouse
Vegetable patch
Pigpen
Chickens

Can you spot these things?
carrots
watch
riding hat
duckling
shoe
This hen is hiding on the farm. Can you find her in every farm scene?
Cows
Stables

Cows like to live in herds with lots of other cows.
Every cow's pattern of spots is different!

Mooooo!
Can you find and color these things?
dragonfly
mouse
sheep
padlock
scarf

Can you spot these things?
candlestick
worm
caterpillar
bone
snail
Cock-a-doodle-doo!
The piglets in the farmyard love to play in the mud!

How many geese can you spot?

Which of the fruits and vegetables can you name?

When they were first discovered, carrots were purple!
Can you spot these things?
squirrel
worm
button
radish
pumpkin

Can you find and color these things?
frog
toothbrush
cupcake
spiderweb
bridle
There are hundreds of types, or breeds, of horses.

Which horse would you like to ride?

Can you spot these things?
washcloth
cucumber
armband
glasses
fan

Rolling in mud is called wallowing.
Mud protects pigs from sunburn!

How many
horse trailers are there?
Can you spot these things?
mouse
glove
wheel
radio
pig

Tractors are slow,
but very strong.

Which sheep has a bare tummy?

Can you find and color these things?
brush
scissors
sweater
sheepdog
cat
In spring the farmer shears his sheep.

How many chicks can you see?
Can you spot these things?
top hat
daffodil
comb
mask
hair clip

Chickens sleep above the ground on a bar called a perch.

When wheat turns golden, it's time for the farmer to cut it.

Can you think of a food that is made from wheat?
Can you find and color these things?
flower
leaf insect
grasshopper
mouse
slug

More to spot

Go back and find these farm scenes!

1

2

3

4

5

6

7

8

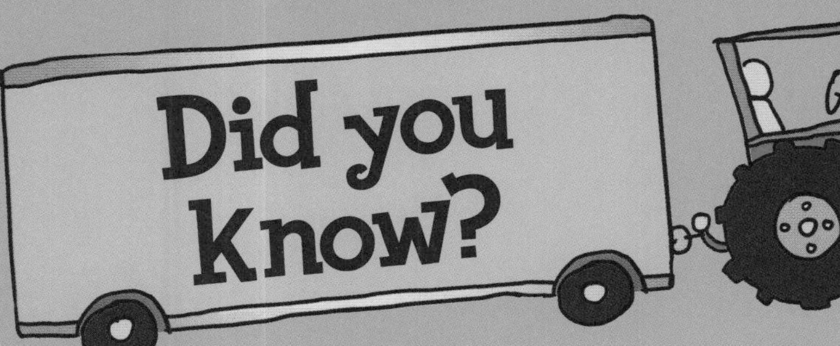

Did you Know?

A chicken can lay about 300 eggs per year. That's almost one a day!

Sheep eat for about seven hours every day.

After cows have swallowed their food, it comes back into their mouths so they can chew it again.

Pigs are very smart and friendly. They make great pets!

A single ant can lift 20 times its body weight. That's like you lifting a tiger!

Who's hiding in the jungle?
Let's step into the rainforest
and find out!
River
Watering hole
Fruit
Treetops
Can you
spot these
things?
pink dolphin
flying frog
okapi
sun bear
tortoise

Thunderstorm
Nighttime
Monkeys
Flowers
Jungle floor
This toucan is hiding in the jungle. Can you find him in every jungle scene?

One of the biggest flowers in the world is the Rafflesia. It's red with spots and it smells horrible!

Can you spot these things?
yellow parrot
bee
gorilla
green spider
purple flower
Can you think of three things that smell nice?

The bright colors of
poison dart frogs warn other
animals that they are
very poisonous!

How many poison dart frogs can you see? Color in all of them!
Can you find and color these things?
caterpillar
beetle
bug
dragonfly
pitcher plant

A crocodile has lots of sharp teeth. Sometimes little birds help to clean them while the crocodile is asleep!

How many snakes can you count?
Can you spot these things?
teddy bear
binoculars
rubber ring
fly-catching frog
butterfly

Howler monkeys are
so loud they can be heard
up to three miles away!

Which monkey looks the funniest?
Can you find and color these things?
glasses
leaf
bow
hair dryer
comb

Orangutans live in the trees. When it rains very hard, they make umbrellas from leaves.

Can you spot these things?
pink frog
parrot
feather
monkey
ladybug
Someone has dropped their binoculars. Can you spot them?

Bats, wild cats, and lots of other jungle creatures come out at night.

Can you count the fireflies?
Can you spot these things?
genet
owl
bat
moth
aardvark

Three-toed sloths spend most of their lives hanging from branches by their long claws. They even sleep like this!
Can you find and color these things?
fruit
baby sloth
iguana
parrot
awake sloth

A sloth can turn its head almost all the way around! How far can you turn yours?

Thousands of
different sorts of fruit
grow in the jungle.
Can you spot these
things?
watermelon
caterpillar
lime
star fruit
blue butterfly

Which fruit would you like to eat?

Some animals, such as okapis and baby tapirs, have spots and stripes. These make them hard to spot among sunlit leaves.

Can you see a big snake on the ground? It's called a boa constrictor.
Can you find and color these things?
spotted beetle
armadillo
rhinoceros beetle
spider
boat

Which group of explorers is different?

Find 10 differences between these two jungle scenes...

Ocean life

Let's dive under the water!

Can you spot these things?
reindeer
baby turtle
stripy fish
diver
blobfish
Beach
Frozen waters
Dolphins
Strange sea creatures
This pink seahorse is hiding under the water. Can you find her in every ocean scene?
Deep sea

More than 1,500 types of fish
live on the Great Barrier Reef
off the coast of Australia.

Can you spot four shells with pearls inside?
Can you find and color these things?
lionfish
coral
crab
butterflyfish
starfish

Octopuses can change their color to blend in with their surroundings.

Can you find five hidden octopuses?
Can you spot these things?
red crab
barracuda
blue mask
shark
green fish

Dolphins are very intelligent. They leap and splash just for fun, and will even make friends with people.
Can you find and color these things?
swordfish
boat
sun hat
palm tree
flag

Would you like to swim with a dolphin?

Baby seahorses eat as many as 3,000 pieces of food a day!

Can you spot these things?
mussels
blue seahorse
yellow fish
red sea cucumber
spotted fish
Seahorses have very good eyesight. They can see forward and backward at the same time!

Whale sharks are the biggest fish in the world. These gentle giants feed on small fish and squid.
Can you find and color these things?
eel
flipper
jellyfish
pufferfish
cleaner fish

Whale sharks are harmless to people!

In winter the ocean around the North Pole freezes. Polar bears cross the ice, hunting for seals.

Can you spot these things?
walrus
narwhal
whale
pinecone
pink fish

The ocean is
home to some very
strange creatures!
Can you find
and color
these things?
blue ribbon eel
ghost fish
monkfish
yeti crab
parrotfish

Who do you think looks the scariest?

Scientists have only explored a tiny part of the underwater world!
In the deep ocean, some creatures glow in the dark!

Can you
spot these things?
anglerfish
vampire squid
red jellyfish
dumbo octopus
frilled shark

Turtles live in the ocean but lay their eggs on the beach. When the baby turtles hatch, they have to crawl to the sea!
Can you find and color these things?
anchor
seagull
seaweed
crab
striped turtle

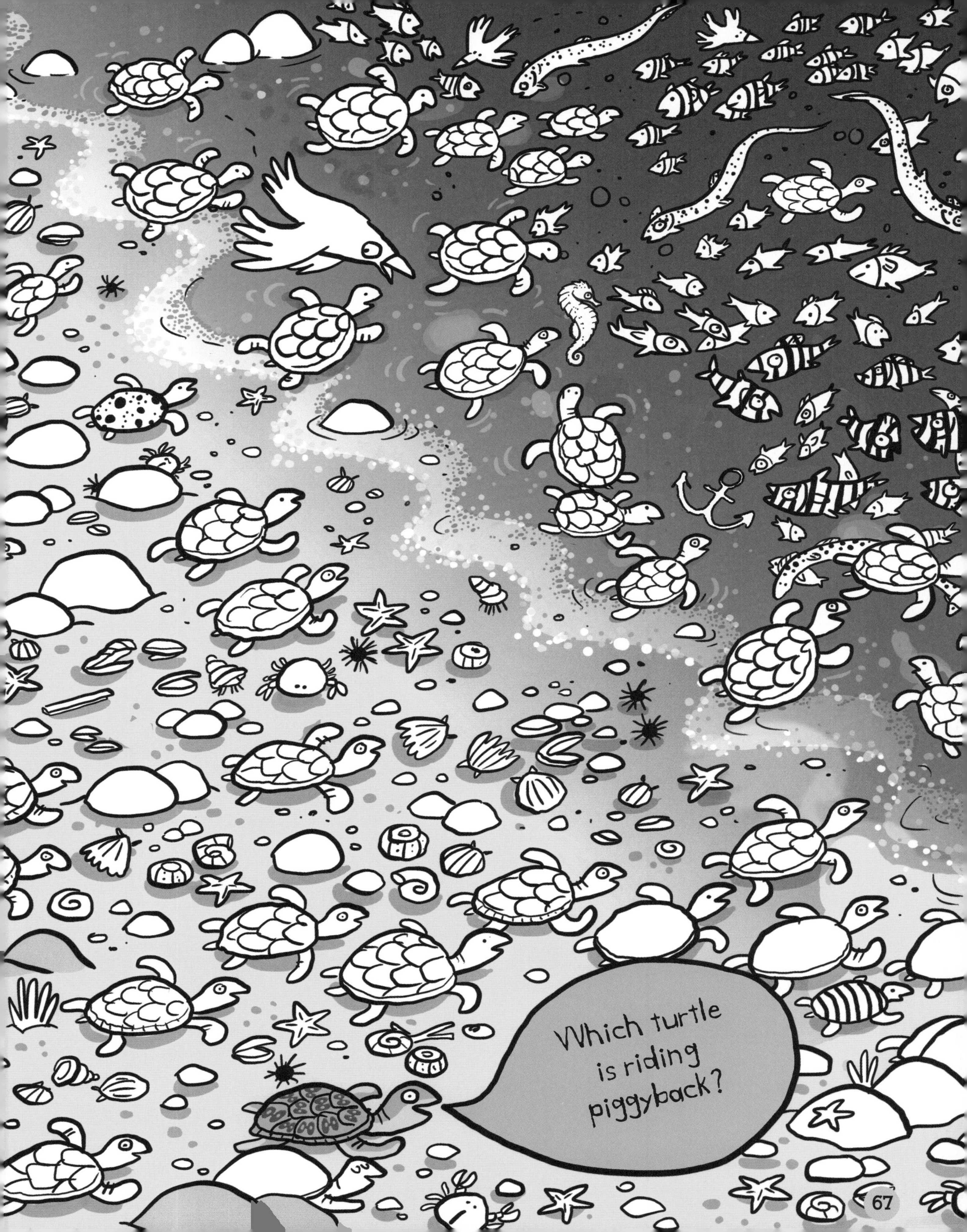
Which turtle
is riding
piggyback?

Which two pairs of fish are the same?

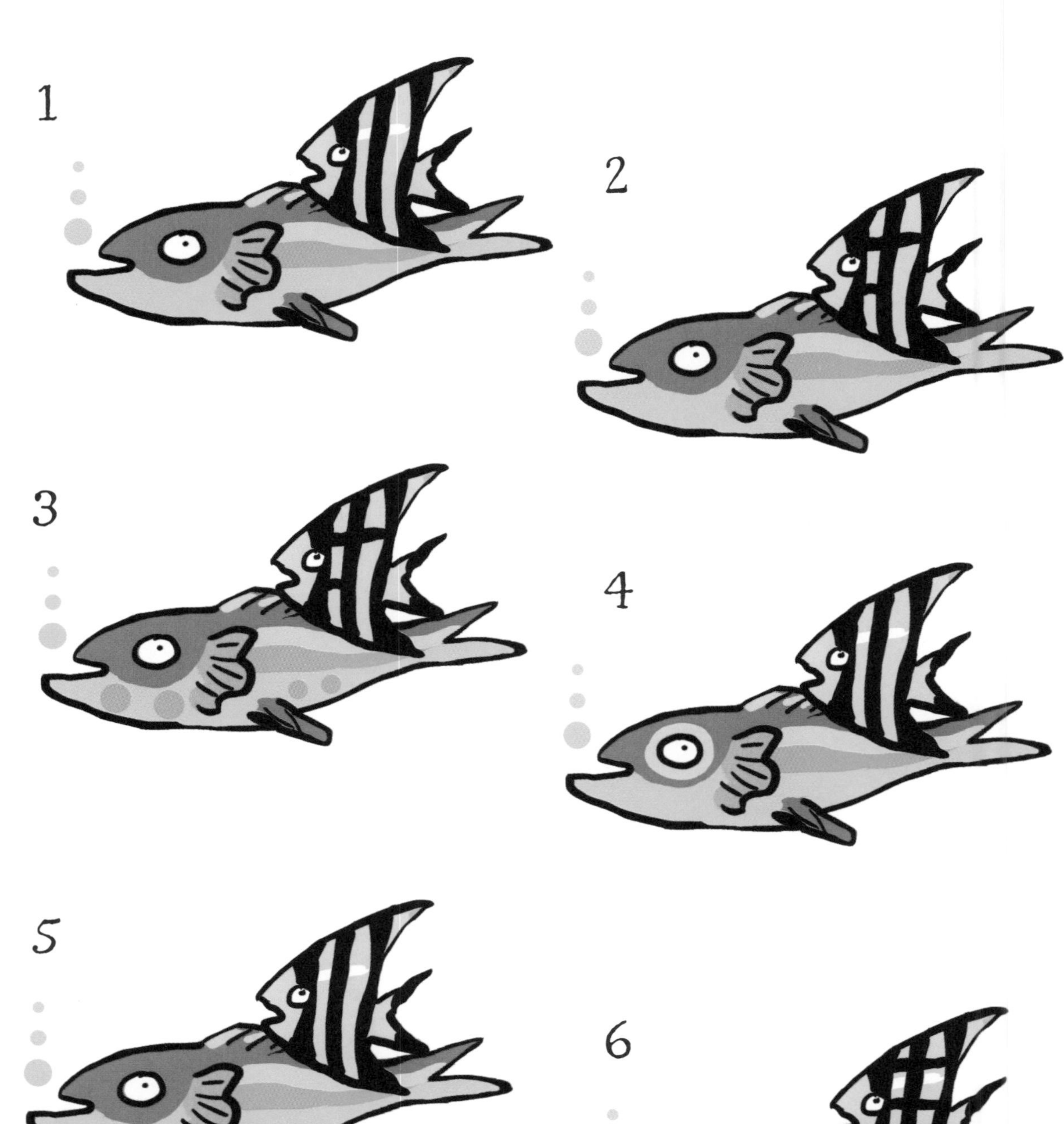

Find 10 differences between these two Arctic ocean scenes...

Big, busy cities!
Let's take a walk across town!
Highway
Apartments
Museum

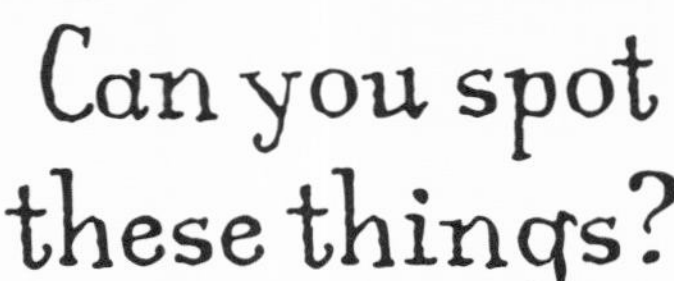

Can you spot these things?

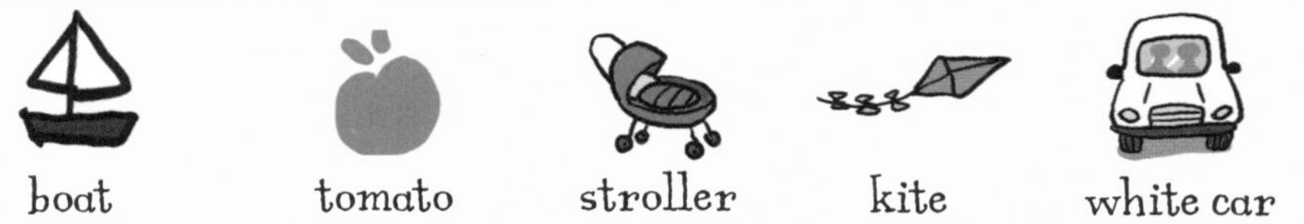

boat

tomato

stroller

kite

white car

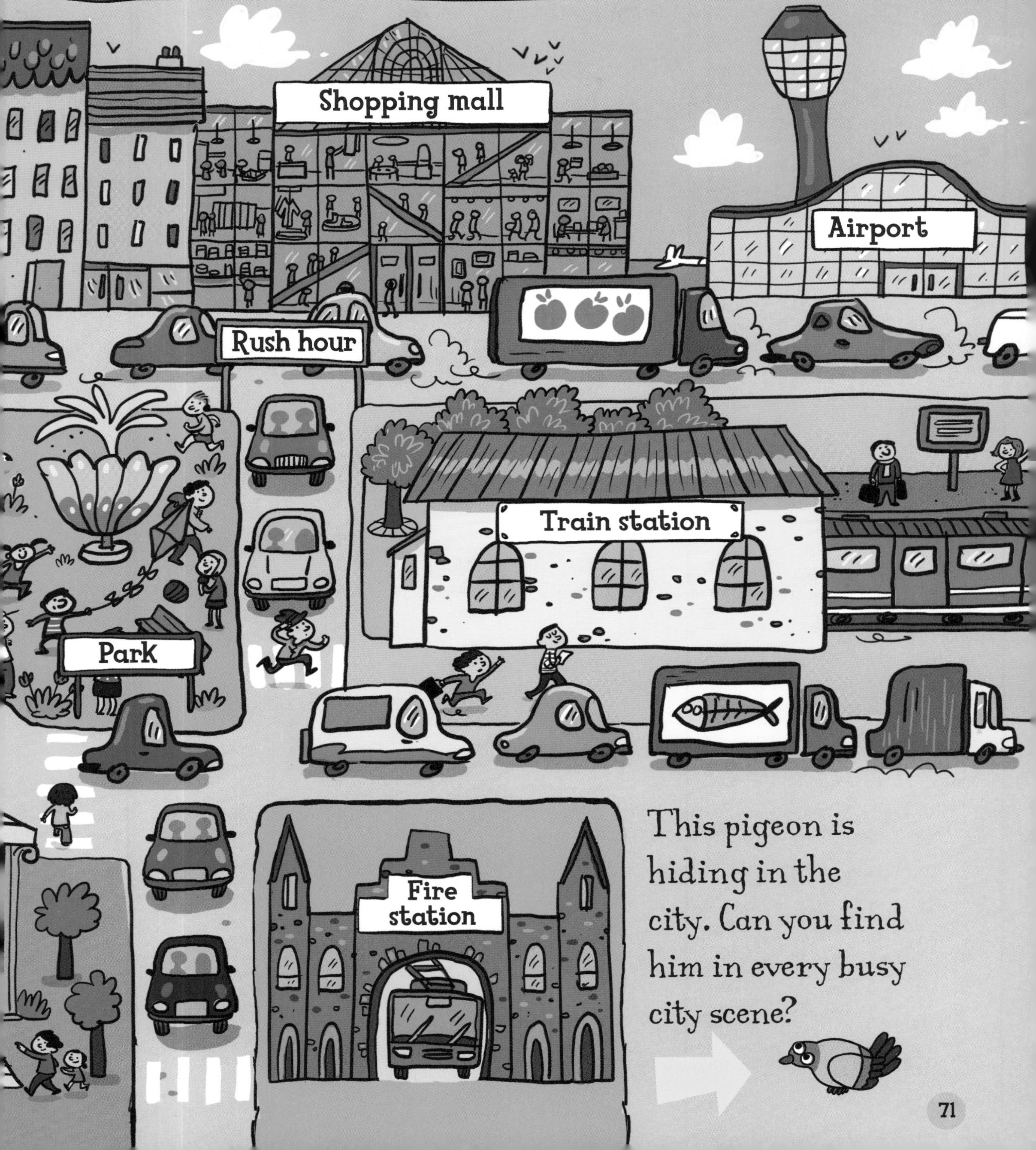

Shopping mall

Airport

Rush hour

Train station

Park

This pigeon is hiding in the city. Can you find him in every busy city scene?

In London, UK, lots of people work in tall buildings called skyscrapers. Very tall cranes are used to build them.

Would you like to drive a crane?
Can you spot these things?
speed boat
hand saw
excavator
hook
bus

Where can I buy a cookie?
Can you spot these things?
pink rabbit
spotted top
hat
garbage can
lamp shade
OPEN

The biggest city shopping malls can have as many as 1,200 shops!

Which vehicle do you think looks the fastest?
Can you find and color these things?
apple
lamp
horse
ham
cap

The longest-ever traffic jam was almost as long as 17 football fields.

The world's cities are getting bigger as more people move into them. Here are some new houses and a playground.

Can you spot these things?
chainsaw
shovel
safety goggles
step ladder
swing seat
CEMENT

Most big cities have an airport close by.

Have you ever been in an airplane?
Can you spot these things?
baby
boots
backpack
dog
laptop
hat
DUTY FREE

At the fire station the crew makes sure the fire engine is ready to go.

How many helmets can you count?

In the museum, you can find out how big dinosaurs really were!
Dinosaurs laid eggs. Can you spot a nest?
HADROSAUR
(Had-roh-sore)
ARCHAEOPTERYX
(Ark-ee-op-ter-ix)
TYRANNOSAURUS
(Tie-ran-uh-sore-us)
ANKYLOSAURU
(An-ki-loh-sore-
STEGOSAURUS
(Steg-uh-sore-us)
Can you spot these things?
cheek spike
nose horn
feathery tail
head crest
frill

PTEROSAUR
(Terra-sore)
TRICERATOPS
(Try-serra-tops)
DIPLODOCUS
(Dip-lo-doh-cus)

Some museums are free to enter. The money they make from selling food and gifts helps them to stay open.

GIFT SHOP
What would you like to buy from the gift shop?
Can you spot these things?
Egyptian pencil case
dinosaur
jug
bananas
slippers
Venetian mask

Millions of people live close together in big cities.

Can you find and color these things?
broom
radio
fish
underpants
trumpet
Where do you and your family live?

Many cities have a theme park with lots of exciting rides such as roller coasters and big wheels.
Which ride would you like to go on?

Can you spot these things?
wheelbarrow
paint brush
train
tool box
bucket

How many dogs can you see?
Can you find and color these things?
drink
newspaper
hat
xylophone
bucket

Tokyo in Japan has more people than any other city!

OPEN
TICKETS
PLATFORM 2
BUSES
Which train is powered by steam?
Can you spot these things?
flowers
suitcase
clock
water bottle
poodle

Trains used to be powered by steam, but today most trains run on diesel or electricity.

Can you spot someone doing the splits?

Can you find and color these things?
striped ball
sign
boat
guitar
balloons
skateboard
People go to city parks to walk, play sports, enjoy nature, and relax.

How many cranes can you see?

The city of San Francisco, California, is the world's largest harbor. It's used by all kinds of boats, from tiny dinghies to massive container ships.

Which apartment block is different?

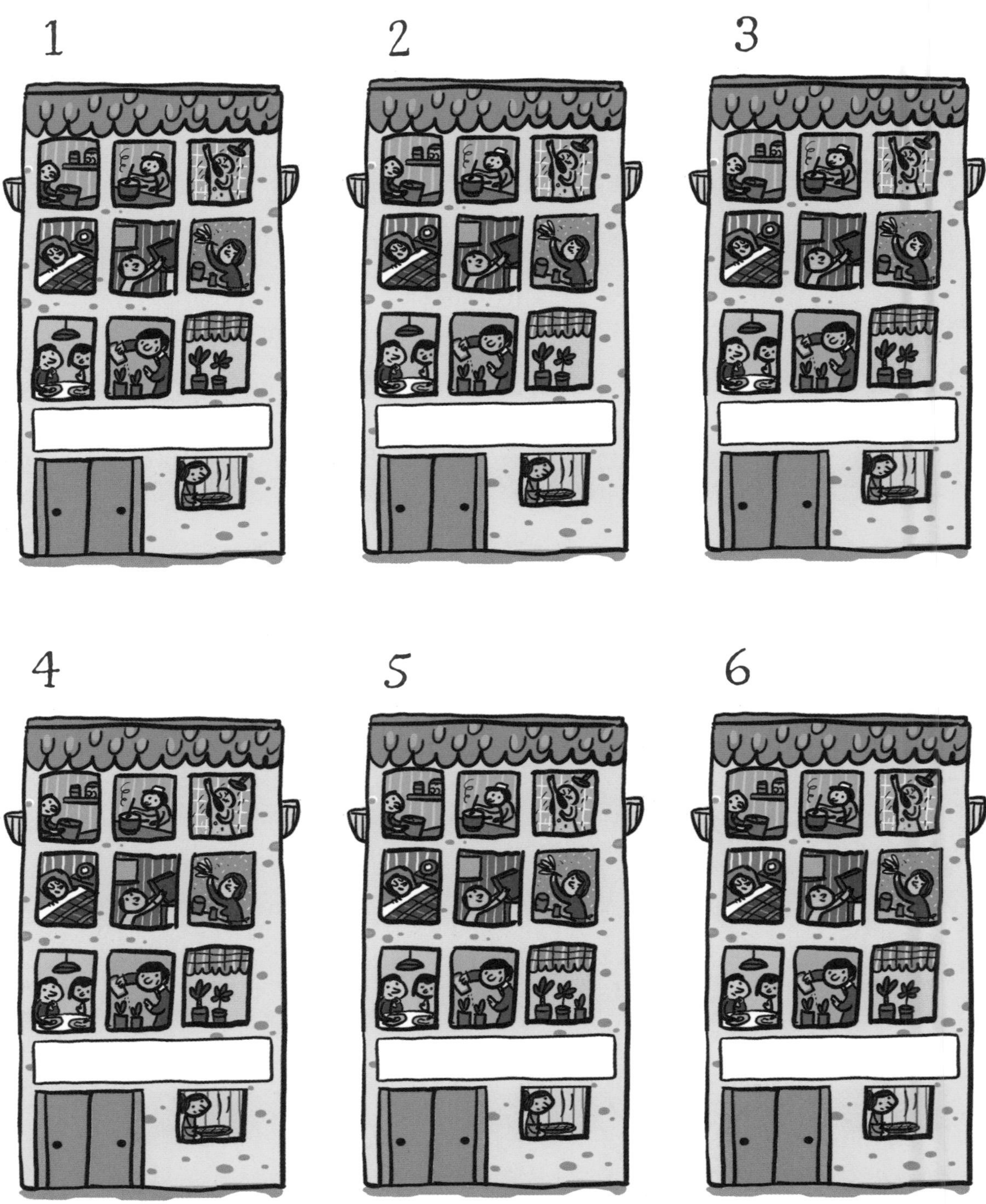

Find 10 differences between these two shopping mall scenes...

A trip to the zoo!
Come and meet the animals!
Butterfly house
Elephants
Penguins
Gorillas
Bugs and reptiles
Aquarium

This meerkat is hiding in the zoo. Can you find her in every zoo scene?

Can you find and color these things?
ball
banana
flower
mirror
rabbit
Find and color all the baby gorillas.

Gorillas live in groups called bands or troops.

Elephants enjoy playing with their friends.
They like to cool off in the water!
Can you spot these things?
butterfly
bird
brush
apple
bow

How many elephants have shut their eyes?

Male lions roar louder than any other big cat!

Which type of big cat do you like best?
Can you find and color these things?
butterfly
zebra
can of cat food
mouse
sunglasses

Can you spot the treasure chest?
Can you find and color these things?
shell
sea sponge
seahorse
fish
eel

A shark can grow thousands of
teeth in its life.

A flamingo's pink
color comes from
the shrimps it eats.

Can you spot the pigeon?
Can you spot these things?
ball of yarn
butterfly
nest
letter
red flower

These glass tanks are home to insects, reptiles, spiders, and amphibians.

Can you find and color these things?

flower

mouse

cup

yarn

glass jar

toy car

Chameleons can change the color of their skin.

Can you spot these things?

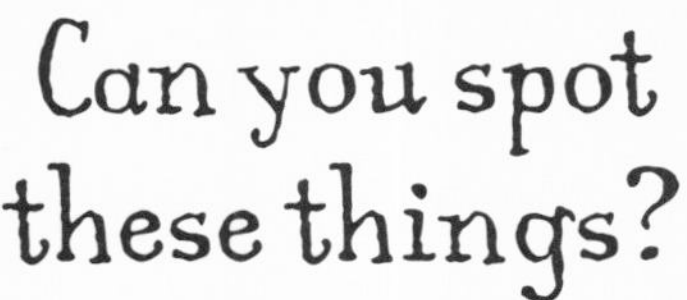
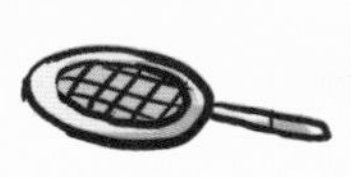
tennis racket

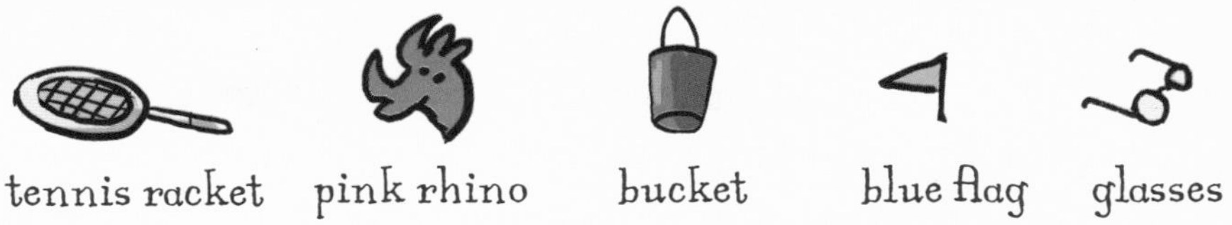

pink rhino

bucket

blue flag

glasses

If wildebeest spot a lion, they all run away together.

Giraffes can run fast on their long legs, but ostriches can run faster!

Butterflies taste with their feet, not their tongues!

Color the butterflies in bright and beautiful colors.
Can you find and color these things?
ladybug with two spots
butterfly
flower
bee on a flower

DAILY PENGUIN
Penguins use their wings like flippers to swim underwater and hunt for fish to eat.
Can you find and color these things?
ribbon
guitar

NO HUMANS
Penguins are birds that can't fly!
ice cream
binoculars
boot

More to color

Finish drawing the pictures using the grids to help you. Then color them in!

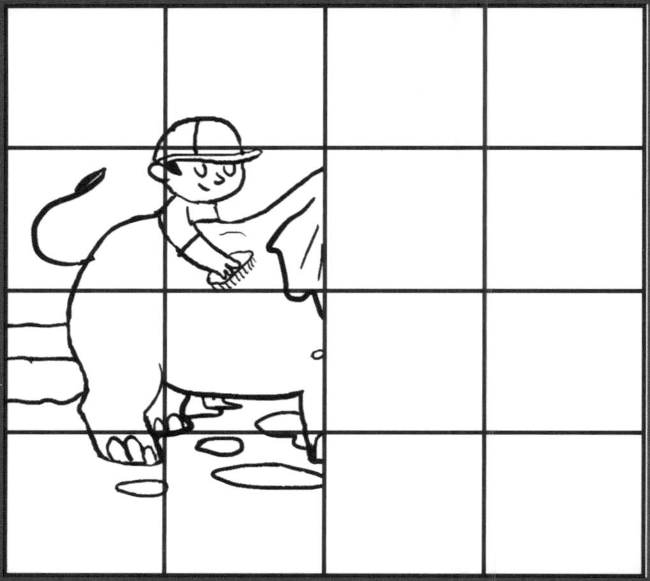

Did you Know?
The tail of a peacock can be over 6 feet (1.8 m) long. That's as long as a lion!
A hammerhead shark's favorite meal is stingray.
Elephants use their trunks to say hello and can even hug each other with them.
Penguins have spines on their tongues.
Tigers can swim up to 3.7 miles (6 km). That's as long as 60 football fields!

Into the garden

There's always lots to do. Let's take a look!

Bees
Lawn
Can you find this pink rabbit hiding in each garden scene?

Bees feed on a sugary liquid called nectar that they find in flowers.

Bees fly to yellow and blue flowers. They cannot see red!
Can you find and color these things?
baseball hat
sunglasses
parachute
snail
bear-shaped bottle

Caterpillars must eat as much as they can before they turn into butterflies.
How many caterpillars can you count?

Can you spot these things?
green bird
rake
spider
snail
faucet

Can you find and color these things?
spider
roses
book
owl
squirrel in nest

Squirrels bury nuts so they have food for the winter, but they often forget where they have put them!

How many pinecones can you count?

Dragonflies are amazing flyers. They can fly straight up and down, and hover in midair.

A dragonfly can spot you creeping up behind it!
Can you spot these things?
fork
apple
toadstool
logs
mosquito

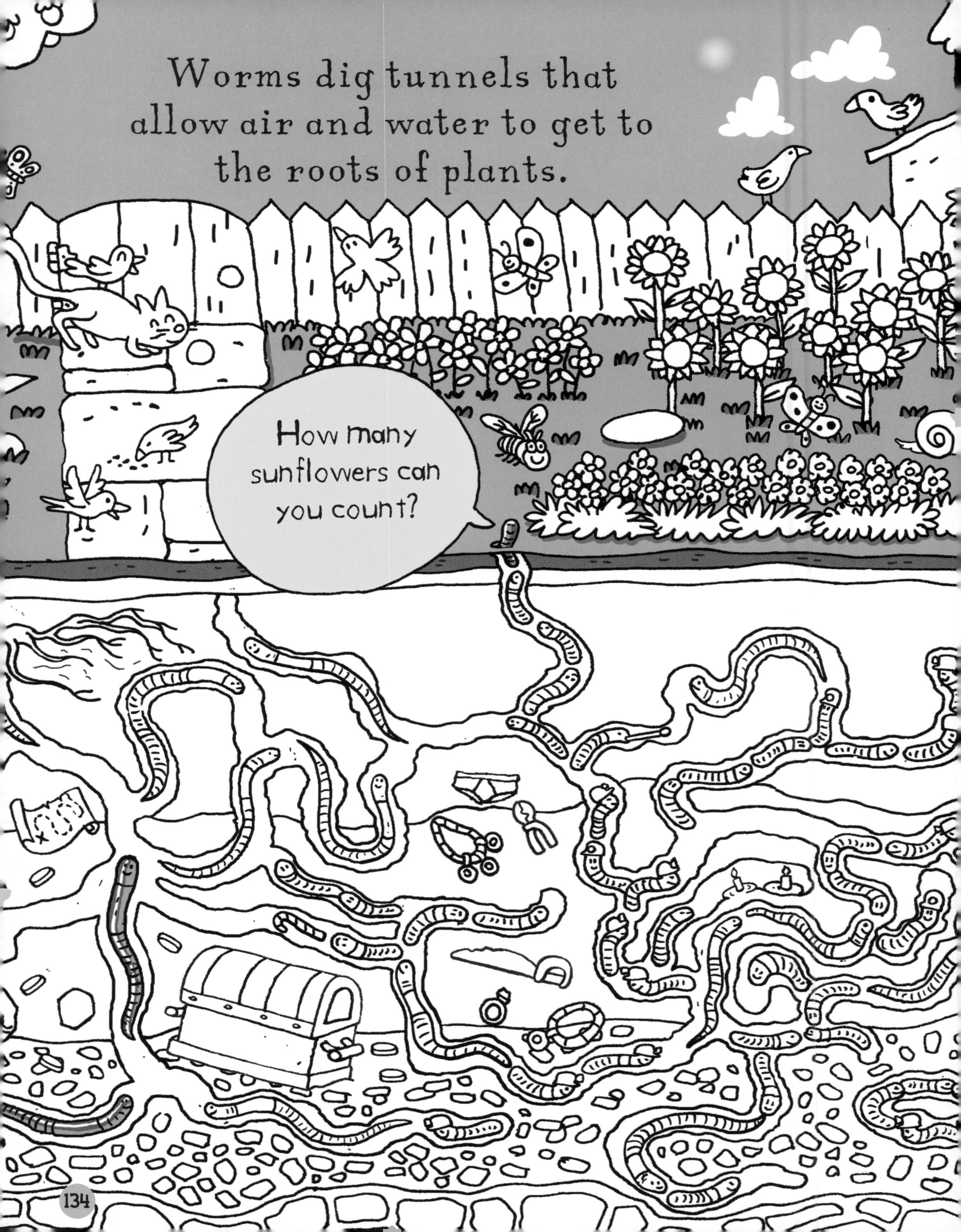
Worms dig tunnels that allow air and water to get to the roots of plants.
How many sunflowers can you count?

Can you find and color these things?
ring
flashlight
underpants
beetle
candy cane

Birds sing different songs to attract a mate, warn of danger, or guard their nest.

Can you spot these things?

chicken

basket

toy plane

red flowers

nesting box

Cats and dogs are the
most popular pets.
Dogs sweat through
their feet. Cats
don't sweat!

Can you find and color these things?
hamster
carrot
canary
tortoise
collar
Which of these pets is your favorite?

If you look out of your window at night, you may see lots of creatures looking for food in the yard!
What noise do I make?

Can you spot these things?
spiderweb
grasshopper
toy car
woodlouse
soccer ball

Ants carry food back to their nest. They may go looking for food up to 30 times a day!

Can you find and color these things?
lemon
bird
jump rope
hat
mouse
Which ant is carrying the biggest load?

More to spot

Go back and find these garden scenes!

1

2

3

4

5

6

7

8

9

Find 10 differences between these two garden scenes...

Dinosaurs everywhere!

Watch out! There are dinosaurs about.

Can you spot these things?

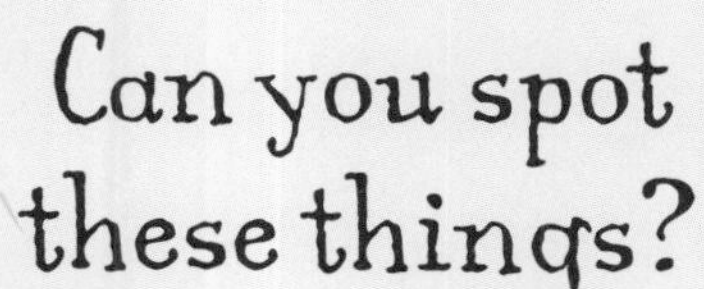
fish

bone

baby dinosaur

feathered dinosaur

green dinosaur

This baby dinosaur is hatching on the island. Can you find him in every dinosaur scene?

Which dinosaur do you like the best?

Although some dinosaurs ate meat, most of them were plant eaters.

Triceratops
(*Try-serra-tops*)
had a big neck frill
and three horns for
fighting enemies.
Can you spot these dinosaurs?
Troodon
(*Troh-oh-don*)
Allosaurus
(*Al-oh-sore-us*)
Dracorex
(*Dray-ko-rex*)
Gastonia
(*Gas-toe-nee-ah*)
Oviraptor
(*Oh-vee-rap-tor*)

How many *Triceratops* can you see?

Mighty *Supersaurus* (*Super-sore-us*) swallowed its food whole. The leaves it ate had to slide all the way down its long neck!

Supersaurus was one of the longest dinosaurs.
Can you find and color these things?
toadstools
dinosaur hatching
butterfly
dinosaur munching
log

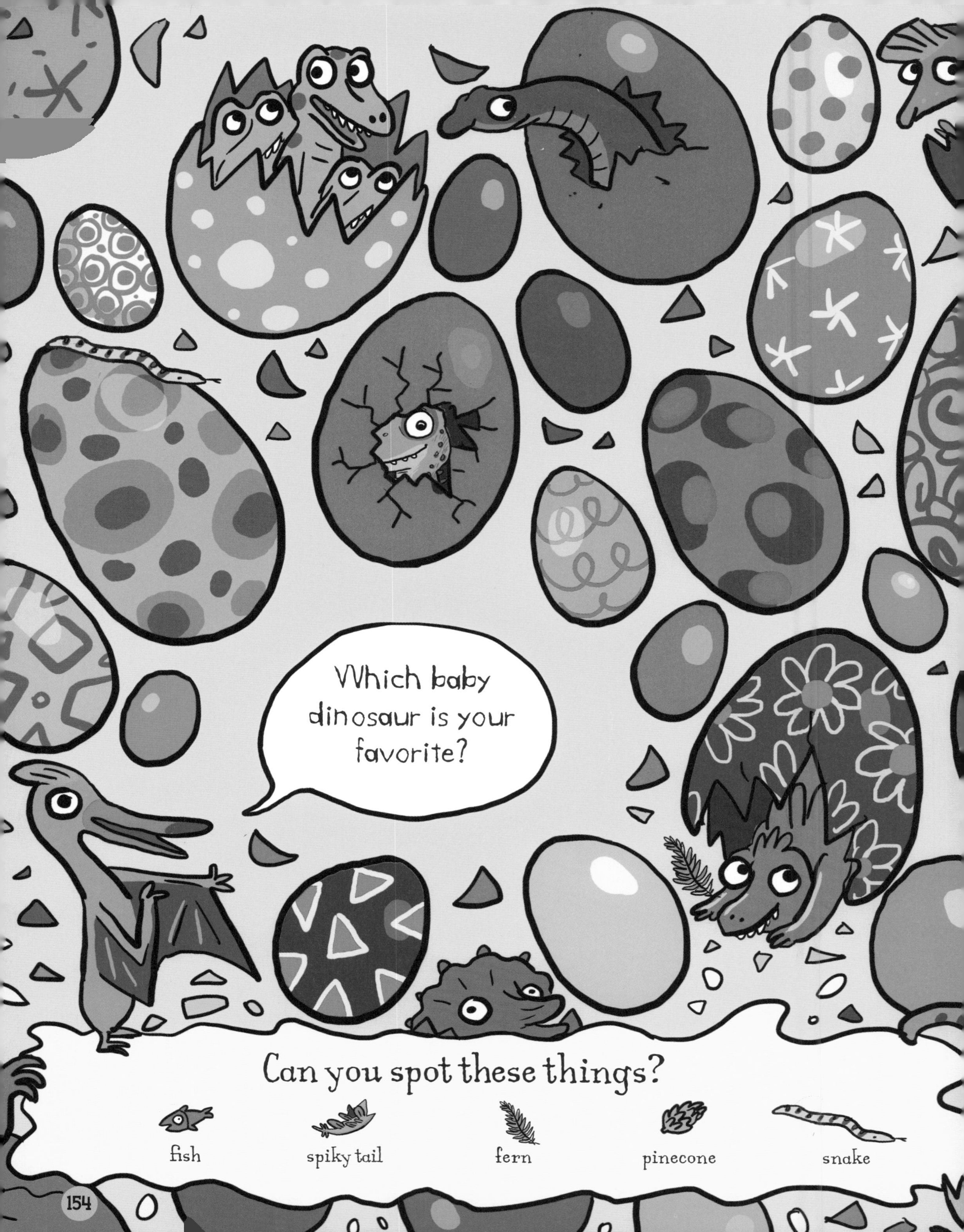
Which baby dinosaur is your favorite?
Can you spot these things?
fish
spiky tail
fern
pinecone
snake

The biggest dinosaur eggs were about as tall as a car tire!

Can you find and color these things?
egg
baby dinosaur
toothbrush
mouse
tooth
The vicious *Velociraptor* (*Vell-oss-ee-rap-tor*) was a small, fast dinosaur with long, curved claws on its feet.

Velociraptors ate other dinosaurs!

Stegosaurus (*Steg-uh-sore-us*) means "roof lizard." It had big, bony plates on its back that looked like roof tiles.

Can you spot these things?
red lizard
palm tree
boat
hat
mirror

Giant pterosaurs (*terra-sores*) flew above the dinosaurs. Some of them were as big as planes!

Which pterosaur is carrying a stone?
Can you find and color these things?
crab
fir tree
mountain
crown of feathers
spider

The sharp-toothed swimmer *Plesiosaurus* (*Plez-io-sore-us*) had four flippers and a long neck.
Can you spot these things?
yellow fish
striped fish
green shell
turtle
squid

Which sea creature looks the scariest?

Can you find and color these things?
teddy bear
bread roll
rake
magnifying glass
cap

How many dinosaur ribs can you see?
Dinosaur fossils give us clues about how dinosaurs lived millions of years ago.

Which *Stegosaurus* is different?

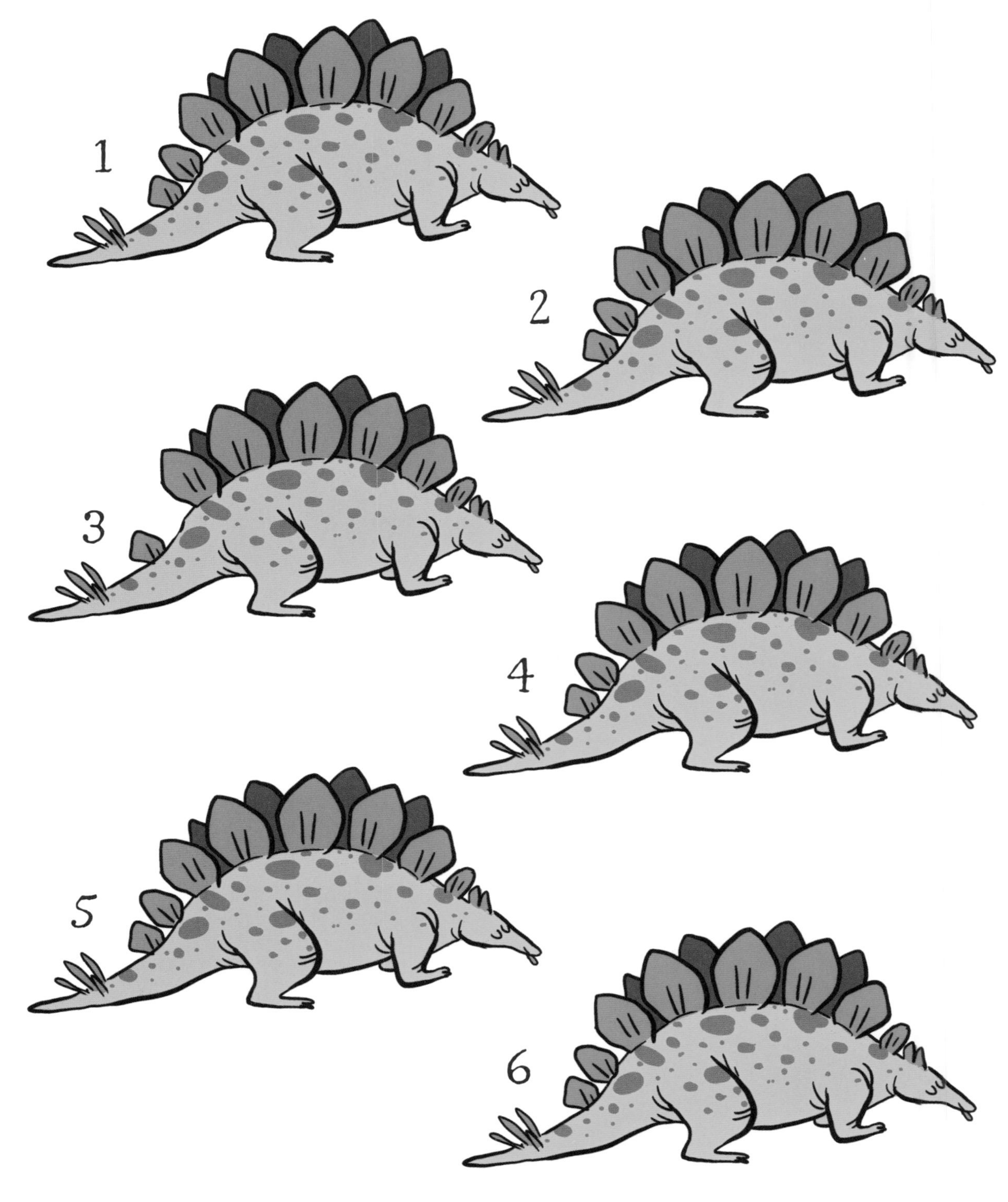

Find 10 differences between these two plesiosaur scenes...

A space adventure!
Let's take a ride across the universe!
Earth
Mars
Our Solar System

Can you spot these things?
tree
rocket
ball
umbrella
alien
Planet Zorgoop!
This alien is hiding in space. Can you find him in every space scene?

Can you find and color these things?
computer
tie
toy spaceship
teddy bear
TV camera
The first person in space was Yuri Gagarin from Russia.

How many astronauts are wearing helmets?

Can you spot these things?
tennis ball
letter
door
spaceship
drawers
alien
Welcome to Planet Zorgoop!

Aliens are creatures from other planets. This alien city looks like lots of fun!

Can you see an alien with four eyes?

UFO stands for unidentified flying object.
Can you find and color these things?
scarf
goggles
necklace
ear muffs
party hat

There's life on this planet!
Shall we land our spaceship?
Can you spot these things?
flower
asteroid
butterfly
controls
spaceship

Did you know,
asteroids are large
chunks of rock?

Uranus
This is our Solar System—the Sun
and eight planets that orbit it.
Sun
Jupiter
Neptune
Earth

Saturn
Mars
Mercury
Venus
Which planet would you like to visit?
Can you find and color these things?
sock
carrot
traffic lights
juice
toothpaste

Can you spot the hot dog?

Can you spot these things?
pink fries
spotted fruit
baby alien
pink mash
potted plant
Where's my blue drink?

Mars is known as the "red planet" because it is covered in red dust and rocks!

Can you spot the tiny alien?
Can you find and color these things?
hammer
flower
sock
glasses
donut

In space everything is weightless, so it floats!

Where are my socks?
Can you find and color these things?
dustpan
night cap
soccer ball
cake
flag

It's time to go home!
Where on Earth shall we land?
Can you spot these things?
octopus
flag
ship
Eiffel Tower
lion

Asia
Europe
Atlantic Ocean
Africa
How many airplanes can you see?

More to color

Finish drawing the pictures using the grids to help you. Then color them in!

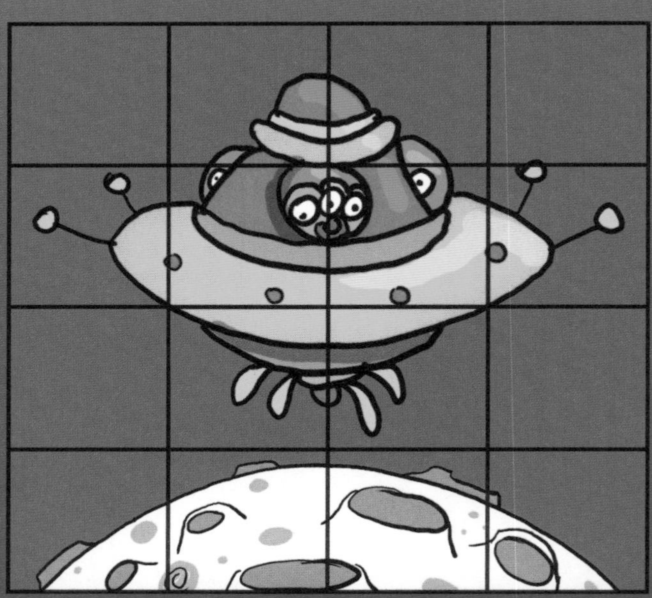

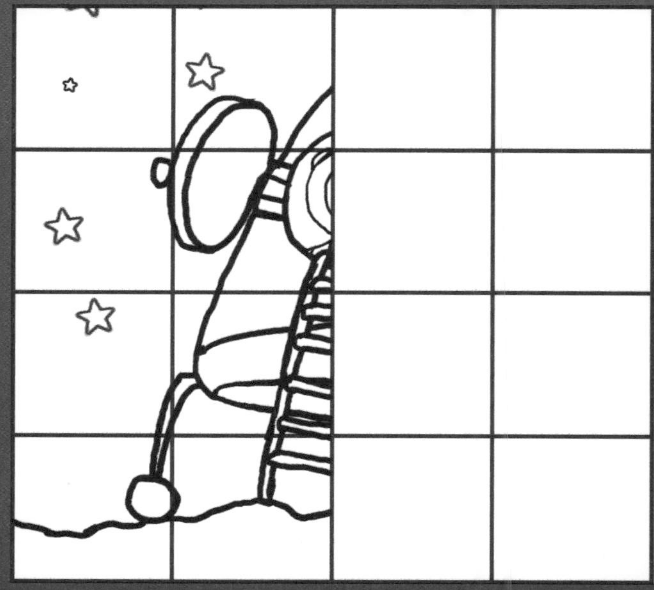

Did you Know?

In 1963, Valentina Tereshkova became the first woman in space. She was 26 years old.

One of the first animals in space was a Russian dog named Laika.

We can see some planets in the night sky because they reflect light from the Sun.

To take off, a rocket needs power to escape Earth's gravity. It burns gas to push away from Earth.

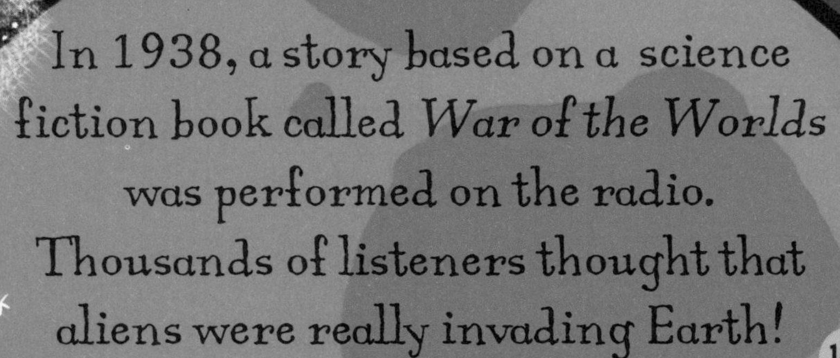

In 1938, a story based on a science fiction book called *War of the Worlds* was performed on the radio. Thousands of listeners thought that aliens were really invading Earth!

Answers

Fun on the farm!

8–9 There are three geese.

16–17 There are six horse trailers.

18–19

20–21 There are five chicks.

23 Many types of bread and pasta are made from wheat, as well as couscous, tortillas, cakes, biscuits, and muffins.

Who's hiding in the jungle?

30–31 There are eleven frogs.

32–33 There are six snakes.

36–37

38–39 There are 24 fireflies.

44–45

46 6 is the odd one out.

47

Ocean life

50–51

52–53

60–61

66–67

68 1 and 5 are the same.

69

Big, busy cities!

74–75

82–83 There are 19 helmets.

84–85

92–93 There are nine dogs.

94–95

96–97

98–99 There are six cranes.

100 5 is the odd one out.

101

A trip to the zoo!

106–107 There are eight elephants with shut eyes.

110–111

112–113

114 A spider has eight legs.

Into the garden

128–129 There are nine caterpillars.

130–131 There are five pinecones.

134–135 There are 14 sunflowers.

136–137 There are five worms.

140 Owl says hoo, hoo!

142–143 The ant with the watermelon is carrying the biggest load.

145

Dinosaurs everywhere!

150–151 There are three *Triceratops.*

160–161

164–165 Fifteen ribs have been uncovered.

166 3 is the odd one out.

167

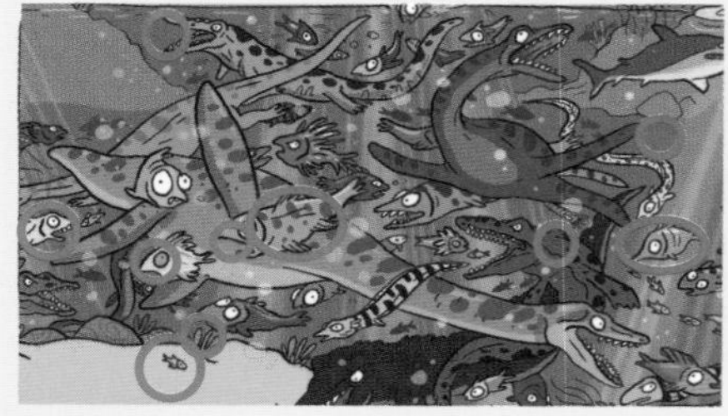

A space adventure!

170–171 Eight astronauts are wearing helmets.

174–175

180–181

182–183

184–185

186–187 There are six airplanes.

More to spot

Did you find us?

PAGES

6–23

28–45

50–67

72–99

104–121

126–143

148–165

170–187